# It's Who You Know

## The One Relationship
## That Makes All the Difference

## Franklin Graham

THOMAS NELSON PUBLISHERS®
Nashville

*A Division of Thomas Nelson, Inc.*
*www.ThomasNelson.com*

Published in Nashville, Tennessee, by Thomas Nelson, Inc.

Scripture quotations noted NKJV are from THE NEW
KING JAMES VERSION. Copyright © 1979, 1980,
1982, Thomas Nelson, Inc., Publishers.

Scripture quotations noted NIV are from the HOLY BIBLE:
NEW INTERNATIONAL VERSION®. Copyright ©
1973, 1978, 1984 by International Bible Society. Used by
permission of Zondervan Publishing House. All rights
reserved.

ISBN 0-7852-6492-2

*Printed in the United States of America*

02 03 04 05 06 PHX 5 4 3 2 1

# It's Who You Know

# Contents

# Introduction

## What's in a Name?

The Name of Jesus stands before, beyond, and after all others.

In the beginning was the Name. At the end will be the Name. In the present time, all things depend upon the Name.

The Name is above all names.

The Name will cause all knees to bow . . . yours, mine . . . for all time.

Do you know the Name?

Are you allied with the Name?

Your life or death depends upon your answers.

\* \* \*

How can any name be that important?

Most of us do not think too much about names—ours or anyone else's.

That certainly was my attitude toward my name for a long time. My family name arrived on American soil long ago by way of my Scottish ancestors—the Grahams actually settled in the Carolinas before the American Revolution.

Growing up, I did not understand or appreciate my family name. Since I was the son of a well-known preacher, Billy Graham, people assumed either the worst or the best about me. The "worst" was that I was a pampered, spoiled brat. The "best," that I was some sort of angelic being living by high standards no one could ever achieve. To be honest, I have never been an angel. If you asked my sisters, they would likely tell you what I really was growing up—a terror.

Later in life, I became more aware that being a Graham and the son of a famous man might have an upside and a downside. The upside was that I was able to meet some interesting people and go to some interesting places. When I was thirteen, President Lyndon Johnson invited my father to spend the night at the White House. Daddy took me along, and guess what? I slept in the Lincoln Bedroom! Since then, I have had the privilege of meeting every U.S. president.

The downside of bearing my family name was people's unrealistic expectations. It was not until I was in my twenties, after fully committing my life to the Lord, that I took much more seriously the privilege and responsibility I had because of my father. I knew that if I did something disgraceful, it would not just embarrass me but bring shame to my family's name, which so many people in the world admired.

I do not want to hurt the name of my earthly father. Yet above all I want to be faithful in bearing the Name of the Lord Jesus Christ.

Again, eternal life or death for each of us depends on our finding protection, refuge, and redemption through the shed blood of Jesus Christ. As the Bible says, "Whoever calls on the name of the LORD shall be saved."[1]

The Apostle John said, "But as many as received Him, to them He gave the right to become children of God, to those who believe in His name."[2]

Believing in the Name of God's only Son is the real issue. From John's statement two thousand years ago until today, a conflict has raged over this Name. The greatest controversy in history was, and still is, this Name.

Why has this Name shaken the very foundations of human society? As you read the chapters ahead, you decide.

# 1

# The Man Behind
# the Name

The Name of Jesus Christ has long ignited strong emotions in human hearts. This is because He affected all of history in His short thirty-three-year life on earth.

Historian Philip Schaff described the overwhelming influence that Jesus had on subsequent history and culture of the world:

This Jesus of Nazareth, without money and arms, conquered more millions than Alexander, Caesar, Mohammed, and Napoleon; without science . . . he shed more light on things human and divine than all philosophers and scholars combined; without the eloquence of schools, he spoke such words of life as were never spoken before or since, and produced effects which lie beyond the reach of orator or poet; without writing a single line, he set more pens in motion, and furnished themes for more sermons, orations, discussions, learned volumes, works of art, and songs of praise than the whole army of great men of ancient and modern times.[1]

One of the great military geniuses of all time, Napoleon I, wrote:

I know men; and I tell you that Jesus Christ is not a man. Superficial minds see a resemblance between Christ and the founders of empires, and the gods of other religions. That resemblance does not exist. There is between Christianity and whatever other religions the distance of infinity. . . . Everything in Christ astonishes me. . . . I search in vain in history to find the similar to Jesus Christ, or anything which can approach the Gospel. Neither history, nor humanity, nor the ages, nor nature, offer me anything with which I am able to compare it or to explain it.[2]

Author H. G. Wells said, "Christ is the most unique person in history. No man can write a history of the human race without giving first and foremost place to the penniless teacher of Nazareth."[3]

Wolfgang Amadeus Mozart, one of the greatest composers and pianists in all of history, said: "It is a great consolation for me to remember that the Lord, to whom I had drawn near in humble and childlike faith, has suffered and died for me, and that He will look on me in love and compassion."

President Theodore Roosevelt, one of the great populist presidents, who, with his swashbuckling style charged San Juan Hill, explored Africa, and took the American flag across the globe, said:

> After a week on perplexing problems it does so rest my soul to . . . come into the house of The Lord and to sing and mean it, "Holy, Holy, Holy, Lord God Almighty." . . . [My] great joy and glory [is] that, in occupying an exalted position in the nation, I am enabled to preach the practical moralities of The Bible to my fellow-countrymen and to hold up Christ as the hope and Savior of the world.

Others, of course, feel much differently. For two thousand years they have scoffed at the Name and mocked those who follow the One who bears it. After all these centuries, just why is the Name so controversial and still stirring such a brew of conflicting passions?

Answering that question is crucial. It is eternally important for you to know much about the Name. This is not just another interesting spiritual topic. An understanding of the Name is the key to all of life.

## WAS JESUS MERELY A RELIGIOUS LEADER?

While the Bible declares that Jesus "is the head of the body, the church" and that "in everything He [has] the supremacy,"[4] many have acknowledged Him as nothing more than a powerful speaker on religious and moral themes. Is this true? Christians who have trusted Jesus personally say no.

How many religions would you guess there are in

the world? Fifty? One hundred? One thousand? Five thousand? The major ones include Christianity, Judaism, Islam, Hinduism, Buddhism, and Shintoism. David Barrett, the editor of the *World Christian Encyclopedia*, stated that there are 9,900 distinct and separate religions in the world.[5] And that number increases every year!

How, then, is it possible for Christians to be so confident about the preeminence of Jesus Christ? Why can't Christians just be content to say that Jesus was simply a good teacher of the past, someone to point the way to God just like so many other religious leaders before and after Him?

The answer about the supreme truth of Christianity revolves around the One who bears the Name—the Lord Jesus Christ. C. S. Lewis, renowned British thinker and writer and one of history's greatest defenders of the Christian faith, wrote:

A man who was merely a man and said the sort of things Jesus said would not be a great moral teacher. He would either be a lunatic—on a level

7

with the man who says he is a poached egg—or else he would be the Devil of Hell. You must make your choice. Either this man was, and is, the Son of God: or else a madman or something worse. You can shut Him up for a fool, you can spit at Him and kill Him as a Demon; or you can fall at His feet and call Him Lord and God. But let us not come with any patronizing nonsense about His being a great human teacher. He has not left that open to us. He did not intend to.[6]

Lewis insightfully pointed out that Jesus couldn't be merely a "good teacher," given what He claimed about Himself in what history records about Him. That option simply isn't available to any thinking person. And what exactly did He claim? The Apostle Paul expressed it well when he wrote the following to the Christians at Colosse:

He is the image of the invisible God, the firstborn over all creation. For by him all things were created: things in heaven and on earth, visible and invisible, whether thrones or powers or rulers or authorities; all things were created by him and for him. He is before all things, and in him all things hold together. And he is the head of the body, the church; he is the beginning and the firstborn from among the dead, so that in everything he might have the supremacy. For God was pleased to have all his fullness dwell in him, and through him to reconcile to himself all things, whether things on earth or things in heaven, by making peace through his blood, shed on the cross.[7]

But is Jesus the only way to God? There is no question more important than this.

In relationship to God, it is not enough to go on what feels right or what we sincerely believe is true. To have life eternal, we must relate to God on His terms, not ours. He is, after all, God. And God Himself said of Jesus, "This is My beloved Son, in whom I am well pleased."[8]

The preeminence of the Lord Jesus Christ is what the writer to the Hebrews was referring to when he wrote:

In the past God spoke to our forefathers through the prophets at many times and in various ways, but in these last days he has spoken to us by his Son, whom he appointed heir of all things, and through whom he made the universe. The Son is the radiance of God's glory and the exact representation of his being, sustaining all things by his powerful word. After he had provided purification for sins, he sat down at the right hand of the Majesty in heaven.[9]

Jesus Himself announced, "I am the way, the truth, and the life. No one comes to the Father except through Me."[10]

Jesus Christ has been the most dominant influence on world history. And the evidence is so overwhelming. The reliability of Scripture, the evidence of the resurrection of Christ, and the common experiences of people worldwide whose lives have been radically changed all speak to the powerful differences between following Jesus Christ and any other "path to God." In fact, Jesus spoke of the other paths when He said, "Enter by the narrow gate; for wide is the gate and broad is the way that leads to destruction, and there are many who go in by it. Because narrow is the gate and difficult is the way which leads to life, and there are few who find it."[11]

Detailed study of the roughly ten thousand religions in the world would expose a smorgasbord of beliefs almost impossible to categorize. When you boil it all down, though, it's very simple. The line of demarcation between the Christian faith and every other religion hinges on this truth: Jesus Christ is uniquely God.

When measured against this standard, the religions of the world pale in comparison with the Name of Jesus. You can accept Him or you can reject Him. You alone will have to confront your own mixed emotions about this Man. The choice is yours.

What will you do with the claims of Jesus Christ?

# 2

# Why Did
# Jesus Come?

Jesus was, and is, the all-time "freedom fighter." Faith in Him and Him alone sets us free from the power of bondage and sin. If you want to be free, follow the Name.

That was the challenge that He gave to all, even to this very day. On the Sabbath, in His hometown of Nazareth, Jesus stood in the synagogue and delivered the "declaration of independence" for all of mankind:

And He was handed the book of the prophet Isaiah. And when He had opened the book, He found the place where it was written:

> "The Spirit of the LORD is upon Me,
> Because He has anointed Me
> To preach the gospel to the poor;
> He has sent Me to heal the broken-
> hearted,
> To proclaim liberty to the captives

And recovery of sight to the blind,
To set at liberty those who are oppressed;
To proclaim the acceptable year of the
    LORD."

Then He closed the book, and gave it back to the attendant and sat down. And the eyes of all who were in the synagogue were fixed on Him. And He began to say to them, "Today this Scripture is fulfilled in your hearing."[1]

With these stunning words, Jesus not only declared that He was the fulfillment of Isaiah's prophecy concerning a coming Savior, but He also promised to free people from everything that oppresses and enslaves the human race.

Jesus said, "Most assuredly, I say to you, whoever commits sin is a slave of sin. And a slave does not abide in the house forever, but a son abides forever. Therefore if the Son makes you free, you shall be free indeed."[2]

The Name of Jesus brings freedom.

Whatever struggles you may face—handicap, weakness, fear, tragedy, or sickness—Jesus came to declare the Good News of hope, liberty, and victory.

Two thousand years have passed since Jesus Christ set His foot on this planet to set captives free. The work of the Holy Spirit continues to this day, freeing men and women from sin's hold on them. Jesus is the liberator and there is eternal freedom in His Name!

## WE NEED HIM NOW
## AS NEVER BEFORE

Recent events have reminded us how precious and hard-won freedom is.

One day a few months ago, I felt as though I were standing on the front porch of hell.

The sight of total destruction, the smell of death, and a thin haze of dust and smoke clung to the air. Ground Zero in Lower Manhattan's Battery Park, on that day, seemed to be the Devil's doorstep.

New York City's famed Mayor Rudy Giuliani

had invited me to give the closing prayer at a family memorial service to honor those who had died in the World Trade Center attacks on September 11.

A temporary platform stood near the mangled steel girders and rubble pit known as "the pile," where just seven weeks earlier, two of the world's tallest towers imploded. After taking my seat on the makeshift platform next to the mayor and other dignitaries and participants, I reflected on the surreal scene.

Behind me smoke—created by seeping gases and fires still not extinguished since the terrorist attacks—spewed from beneath pieces of concrete, rebar, glass, and other refuse. Hoses from fire trucks streamed water into the cauldron, the spray turning to steam that mingled with smoke from the fires. A fine, nearly imperceptible dust settled on my hair, skin, and clothing.

The most hideous invasion of my senses, though, was the stench from still-burning jet fuel and the incineration of hundreds of pulverized bodies.

An American flag hung from a pole in the center of the pile. On a nearby building, a sign read, "We Will Never Forget." That is why we were there: to help remember the dead. Not just firemen, policemen, and tower residents or visitors had perished in the collapse of the buildings. Pilots, flight attendants, passengers—all had fallen into this common grave. Every person who died that tragic day left behind families who now grappled with loss, grief, and unanswered questions.

I could not shake the thought: *This is a picture of hell—the bleak devastation, unquenchable fire, and stench of death.* The grim hopelessness made me shudder.

That day, October 28, work had stopped for the first time at Ground Zero since September 11, and firemen and others laboring in the rubble stood, heads bare, hard hats clutched to their hearts.

The service began with an honor guard marching in the colors. The national anthem was sung by a New York police officer named Daniel Rodriguez. Music and prayers were interspersed. Since this was

19

an interfaith service, representatives of Islam, Judaism, and Christianity participated, and Renee Fleming of the Metropolitan Opera sang "Amazing Grace."

As I watched and listened, I yearned to offer words of hope to these thousands of hurting families. They had lost mothers, fathers, husbands, wives, sons, daughters, brothers, sisters—dear friends, and no one could bring them back.

Before delivering the benediction, I said, "Today, I stand before you as a minister of the Christian faith."

And then I prayed:

Our Father, which art in heaven,
Hallowed be Your Name,
And hallowed is the ground upon which we
    stand,
Your kingdom come, Your will be done, on
    earth as it is in heaven.
We come to You this day to seek Your help,
    Your mercy, and Your grace.

We pray today that You will surround these
    families with Your love and that
You will comfort them during this time of
    great personal loss . . .
God is our refuge and strength,
A very present help in trouble.[3]
But those who wait on the LORD
Shall renew their strength;
They shall mount up with wings like eagles,
They shall run and not be weary,
They shall walk and not faint.[4]


As we grieve today we are reminded of Your grief
and the sacrifice You made for all mankind when
You sent Your Son, Jesus Christ, to this earth to
die for our sins on Calvary's cross, and the hope
that we have through the power of His Name.
What hope is there outside of the Name of the
Lord Jesus Christ?

For I am persuaded that neither death nor life,
nor angels nor principalities nor powers, nor things
present nor things to come, nor height nor depth,

nor any other created thing, shall be able to separate us from the love of God which is in Christ Jesus our Lord.[5]

As I concluded my prayer and looked into the faces of the thousands in front of me, I wished I could do something more, as the grief and pain were overwhelming.

Hell is going to be *eternity* filled with grief and pain, an unquenchable fire, according to the Bible. I could not help but think of the life that we have now and the breath that God has given us. On that September day, not one of the people who died could have imagined that his life would come to such an abrupt and tragic end. It is important that all of us live our lives for Him in the knowledge of His truth and through faith in the Name of His Son; for we never know when our lives will end.

I want to ask you a pointed question: If you had been in one of the World Trade Towers that morning of 9/11, would you have been ready for death? Most of us do not dwell on the thought of death. A visit to Ground Zero causes one to give it some thought. Whether God blesses us with a long life or a short life, there is one thing we all have in common—the grave. Eventually, whether in a tragedy like that of the World Trade Center, from cancer in a hospital bed, or a heart attack in our sleep, we all will face death someday. Do you know your eternal destiny?

You can find freedom from the fear of death in the Name of the Lord Jesus Christ.

# 3

# Seizing
# Hope

I have shared with you some important things about the Name. But knowledge about God never saved anyone. It is not enough to know the story of Jesus. You must know Him personally.

The Bible makes it very clear that God loves us. He cares for us and He wants us to live our lives to the fullest. But for most people, there is emptiness in their lives that they can't explain. Something is missing. They search for it through various religions, through relationships, through the acquisition of things that money can buy, but that emptiness is still in the pit of their souls. There is a vacuum inside all of us—it can be filled only by God when we come into a right relationship with Him.

We can have a relationship with Him. How? Through His Son, Jesus Christ. He is the mediator between God and man. He is not still hanging on a Roman cross. He is alive in heaven—and He loves you. You can have a new life of meaning and purpose, free from guilt. How does that occur? I want to pose a few simple questions that will clarify the facts concerning the most important decision any person will ever make.

Do you feel that something is missing deep down in your very soul?

Do you feel an emptiness that you cannot explain—sometimes a loneliness—even though you may be in the midst of a crowd?

Most people do. In moments when we are most thoughtful about the meaning of life, there is a craving for something more. At its core, this is a longing to know God intimately. Often people try to fill this emptiness with other things—like alcohol, drugs, food, sexual adventures. The list is long. However, none of these can fill this emptiness, or take away this inner loneliness. Nothing can supply the hope we lack.

The truth is that God wants to supply what is missing deep inside your soul. He wants to have a relationship with all of us. Each one of us must make a choice to let God into our lives.

We need to understand what it takes to have a

right relationship with God; for one day, we will all stand before Him.

What separates you from God? What causes that emptiness in your life?

It is sin.

In today's tolerant culture where "anything goes," many do not understand what sin means. Sin is breaking God's laws. When you disobey God's laws, it separates you from Him.

No matter how hard we try, none of us are able to live life without breaking God's laws. The Bible says: "For all have sinned and fall short of the glory of God"[1] and "the wages of sin is death."[2] This is the price, this is the penalty . . . this is the sentence. The Supreme Judge—God Himself— has proclaimed that all of mankind is guilty. Everyone has a sin problem. There is no escaping this because God is morally perfect and "holy," and He demands that anyone who comes near Him must be holy too.

So how do we as sinners ever solve this dilemma? God's answer comes through the perfect life,

death, and resurrection of a substitute sacrifice—
the Lamb of God, His Son, the Lord Jesus Christ—
for our sins. He is the One who paid our debt of
sin. We could not possibly pay it.

The Bible tells us, "God so loved the world
that He gave His only begotten Son, that whoever
believes in Him should not perish but have ever-
lasting life."[3]

And that "whoever" is you and me. Jesus is the
only way to God, because He is the only One in
history to take sin's penalty for you and me. Buddha
did not die for our sins; Muhammad did not die for
our sins. No one paid the debt of sin for us except
the Lord Jesus Christ—He shed His blood on
Calvary's cross, went to the grave, and rose again on
the third day. The only way we can come to God is
by faith through His Son and Him alone.

Jesus is the only door we can pass through to
meet God the Father.

Do you believe? Are you willing to trust Jesus
Christ as your personal Savior? What is your
response?

Do not put off making a decision for Christ. The Bible says, "Behold, now is . . . the day of salvation."[4]

"[God] desires all men to be saved and to come to the knowledge of the truth. For there is one God and one Mediator between God and men, the Man Christ Jesus, who gave Himself a ransom for all."[5]

We must all put our faith in Jesus Christ. The Bible says that "Christ Jesus came into the world to save sinners."[6] Salvation is free to anyone who calls on the Lord Jesus Christ and repents of his sin. It is a gift from God that one can accept. The Bible says, "The gift of God is eternal life in Christ Jesus our Lord."[7]

Because of our sin, we are condemned and sentenced to death; but God offers us a pardon through receiving His Son, Jesus Christ, by faith. The point is that you have to be willing to accept the pardon.

"How do I do that?" you may ask. "How can I trust this Name above all names and experience a new and vibrant life, free from guilt and shame?"

It is simple.

First, you must be willing to confess your sins to God, ask Him for forgiveness, and tell Him that you want to change and turn from the sinful life you have been living.

Next, by faith, ask Jesus Christ to come into your life, take control of your life, and to be the Lord of your life.

Then, follow Him from this day forward by obeying Him and reading His instructions found in His Word, the Holy Bible.

If you are willing to do that, God will forgive you and cleanse you. He will give you a new life and a new beginning. As you close this book, you can have the assurance that you have been saved and that one of these days, when death comes for you, you will have nothing to fear. You will know that for eternity you will be safe in the presence of the King of kings and Lord of lords.

If your desire is to accept Christ as your Savior now, just pray this prayer:

Dear God, I am a sinner. I am sorry for my sins. Forgive me. I believe that Jesus Christ is Your Son. I believe that Jesus Christ died for my sins. I want to invite Him into my life. I want to trust Him as my Savior and follow Him as my Lord, from this day forward, forever more. In Jesus' Name. Amen.

If you have prayed that prayer and meant it, I want you to know that God has forgiven you and cleansed you. Your name is now recorded in the Lamb's Book of Life. This is the record of everyone in history who has trusted the Savior. Your name is written there and it can never be erased.

You have just taken hold of an eternal hope: Jesus our Savior.

# 4

# The Name Above All Names

The brilliant and intense Jewish man—in chains, busily writing letter after letter in his Roman jail cell—understood the magnificence of the Name.

The Apostle Paul, in one affectionate note to some old friends in another city, wrote joyfully about why the Name of Jesus reigns above all others:

And being found in appearance as a man, He humbled Himself and became obedient to the point of death, even the death of the cross. Therefore God also has highly exalted Him and given Him the name which is above every name, that at the name of Jesus every knee should bow, of those in heaven, and of those on earth, and of those under the earth, and that every tongue should confess that Jesus Christ is Lord, to the glory of God the Father.[1]

While our King and Lord waits for the moment when the Father will end human history and authorize Jesus to return—this time not as a humble baby but in the clouds, where "every eye will see Him"[2]—Jesus sits in a place of honor at the right hand of God the Father. He is not idle! Jesus came as a servant and He is still serving today by interceding on our behalf, at His Father's right hand, through prayer.

"But [Jesus], because He continues forever, has an unchangeable priesthood. Therefore He is also able to save to the uttermost those who come to God through Him, since He always lives to make intercession for them."[3]

Not only is He making intercession for us, He is also preparing us a place. Jesus said:

Let not your heart be troubled; you believe in God, believe also in Me. In My Father's house are many mansions; if it were not so, I would have told you. I go to prepare a place for you. And if I go and prepare a place for you, I will come again and receive you to Myself; that where I am, there you may be also.[4]

Someday—could it be today?—the trumpet will sound. In Jesus' own words, here's what will happen: "When the Son of Man comes in His glory, and all the holy angels with Him, then He will sit on the throne of His glory. All the nations will be gathered before Him."[5]

Our God is a gracious and patient Father, but when He lowers the curtain on mankind's story, the play will be over.

As Paul wrote in that letter to his friends at Philippi, every knee will bow and every tongue will confess, "Jesus Christ is Lord."

All knees will bow and every tongue will confess, including:

Abraham, the pharaohs, Moses, Mary and
    Joseph, the disciples
John the Baptist, the Pharisees, Herod, Pilate,
    the Apostle Paul

Roman emperors, Alexander the Great,
    Constantine
Winners and losers
Columbus, Cortes, Perry, Lindberg, Armstrong
Popes, Muhammad, Mahatma Gandhi, Mother
    Teresa
Washington, Lincoln, Roosevelt, Kennedy,
    Reagan
Kings, queens, princes, and princesses
George Wishart, Cassie Bernall, and all martyrs
    wearing their white robes
Babe Ruth, Tiger Woods, Joe Montana,
    America's Cup winners
Mark McGwire, Muhammad Ali
Abortionists and anti-abortionists
Stalin, Hitler, Lenin, Mao, Pol Pot, Bin Laden
Members of the nearly ten thousand religions
Construction workers and doctors
Frank Sinatra, Cher, Michael Jackson,
    Madonna
Marilyn Monroe, Jimmy Stewart, Mel Gibson,
    Julia Roberts

Martin Luther and Martin Luther King

Millionaires and misfits

Carnegie, Vanderbilt, Rockefeller, Walton, Gates

Moonshiners, mafia, drug lords, pushers, and
    addicts

Bunyan, Shakespeare, Hemingway, Lewis,
    Grisham

Pornographers, prostitutes, philanthropists, and
    pedophiles

Larry King, Barbara Walters, David Letterman,
    Tom Brokaw

Patriots and terrorists

Van Gogh, Michelangelo, Picasso, Rockwell

Saddam Hussein, Yasir Arafat

Golda Meir, David Ben Gurion, Ariel Sharon

Rachel the Israeli victim and Ayat the suicide
    bomber

Lawyers and longshoremen

Mozart, Beethoven, Gershwin, Lennon

Skeptics and mockers

Voltaire, Freud, Darwin, Madeline Murray
    O'Hare

Billy and Ruth Graham

Franklin Graham

Your boss and your neighbor

Your spouse and your child

You

Every knee will bow and every tongue will confess, "Jesus Christ is Lord."

Dear friends of our family, Bill and Gloria Gaither, years ago penned words that say it so well:

Jesus, Jesus, Jesus,

There's just something about that Name

Master, Savior, Jesus,

like the fragrance after the rain . . .

Jesus, Jesus, Jesus,

let all heaven and earth proclaim

kings and kingdoms will all pass away

but there's something about that Name.

Jesus, the mere mention of His Name

can calm the storm, heal the broken, and
   raise the dead . . .
At the Name of Jesus
   I've seen sin-hardened men melt, Derelicts
      transformed
   the lights of hope put back into the eyes of
      a hopeless child . . .
At the Name of Jesus
   hatred and bitterness turn to love and
      forgiveness
   arguments cease . . .
I've heard a mother softly breathe His Name
   at the bedside of a child delirious from fever
   and I've watched that little body grow quiet
   and the fevered brow cool . . .
I've sat beside a dying saint
her body racked with pain
who in those final fleeting seconds summoned
      her last ounce of having strength
to whisper earth's sweetest Name, Jesus, Jesus . . .
Emperors have tried to destroy it
philosophies have tried to stamp it out

Tyrants have tried to wash it from the face of
    the earth
  with the very blood of those who claimed it
  yet still it stands . . .
And there shall be that final day
  when every voice that has ever uttered a
    sound
  every voice of Adam's race
  shall raise in one great mighty chorus
  to proclaim the Name of Jesus . . .
For in that day every knee shall bow
  and every tongue shall confess
  that Jesus Christ is Lord.
So you see . . .
  it wasn't by mere chance
  that caused the angel one night long ago
  to say to a virgin maiden
His Name shall be called
Jesus, Jesus, Jesus . . .
You know . . .
  there is something about that Name.[6]

One day we will all stand before Jesus, either as our Savior or our judge. I don't know about you, but I am ready to face the One who is owed all the glory and honor, the One who bears the Name—Jesus.

# Notes

INTRODUCTION
1. Acts 2:21 NKJV.
2. John 1:12 NKJV.

CHAPTER 1
1. Internet, *www.ccci.org,* "Who Is Jesus?" Accessed on 28 April 2002.
2. Josh McDowell, *Evidence That Demands a Verdict,* Volume 1 (Nashville: Thomas Nelson Publishers, 1979), 106.
3. Calvin Miller, *The Book of Jesus* (New York: Simon & Schuster, 1996), 290.
4. Colossians 1:18 NIV.
5. Toby Lester, "Oh, Gods!" *Atlantic Monthly,* February 2002, 38.
6. C. S. Lewis, *Mere Christianity* (New York: Macmillan Publishing Co., Inc., 1952), 56.
7. Colossians 1:15–20 NIV.
8. Matthew 3:17 NKJV.
9. Hebrews 1:1–3 NIV.
10. John 14:6 NKJV.
11. Matthew 7:13–14 NKJV.

CHAPTER 2

1. Luke 4:17–21 NKJV.
2. John 8:34–36 NKJV.
3. Psalm 46:1 NKJV.
4. Isaiah 40:31 NKJV.
5. Romans 8:38–39 NKJV.

CHAPTER 3

1. Romans 3:23 NKJV.
2. Romans 6:23 NKJV.
3. John 3:16 NKJV.
4. 2 Corinthians 6:2 NKJV.
5. 1 Timothy 2:4–6 NKJV.
6. 1 Timothy 1:15 NKJV.
7. Romans 6:23 NKJV.

CHAPTER 4

1. Philippians 2:8–11 NKJV.
2. Revelation 1:7 NKJV.
3. Hebrews 7:24–25 NKJV.
4. John 14:1–3 NKJV.
5. Matthew 25:31–32 NKJV.
6. "Jesus: There's Just Something About That Name," words by Bill and Gloria Gaither. Used by permission.

In his autobiography, Franklin Graham tells
his story of how God has taken his life and
turned it into His Glory. Elizabeth Dole
says, "Franklin has provided a very
thoughtful and provocative account of how
a young man develops and matures in his
faith as the son of one of the world's most
respected and admired spiritual leaders."

*Rebel with a Cause*

**ISBN 0-7852-7170-8**

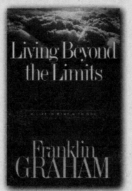

In Living Beyond the Limits, Franklin
Graham focuses on God's principles and
promises essential to a full life. He relates
real-life examples of men and women who
have put God's Word into practice under
some of the most challenging circumstances
imaginable. You'll be amazed by their
stories. You'll also be stirred and
challenged as never before.

*Living Beyond the Limits*
ISBN 0-7852-7184-8

The Name shouts out a choice: *Whom will
you serve, give your life to, depend upon?*
Rebellious, self-willed, sinful people want to
retain the right to decide themselves what
way they will take. Jesus denies this option.
Speaking on His behalf, the apostle Peter
said, "There is no other name under heaven
given among men by which we must
be saved."

Jesus is gentle, but He is not weak.
He loves the sinner
but is absolutely intolerant of sin.
He is not a negotiator. He is Lord!

**ISBN 0-7852-6522-8**